Confessions of a Captured Angel

Confessions
of a
Captured Angel

Neil Carpathios

Terrapin Books

© 2016 by Neil Carpathios

Printed in the United States of America
All rights reserved.

No part of this book may be reproduced in any manner, except for brief quotations embedded in critical articles or reviews.

Terrapin Books
4 Midvale Avenue
West Caldwell, NJ 07006

www.terrapinbooks.com

ISBN: 978-0-9969871-5-8
LCCN: 2016938516

First Edition

Cover art by Carole Carpathios

for my mother, my angel

Contents

I

Owner's Manual	3
The Captured Angel Confesses	4
Sixth Birthday: The Transparent Model Man	6
The Secret Power	7
Early Lesson	11
Spirits	13
Sweetness	16
Death and Birth	18
Siste Viator	19
My Father's Death Turns One Year Old	21
The Sweat Mark	22
The Captured Angel Comments on Death	24

II

While You Were Gone Getting Tomatoes for Our Salad	29
Upon Discovering My Daughter's Tattoo	30
The Artist	32
I Drive Through a Blizzard for a Cup of Tea	34
Miscarriage	36
Kitchen Jeopardy	38
The Captured Angel Comments on Blame	40
As the Gods Booby-Trap Love	42
In Praise of Surrealism	43
In Praise of the Ordinary	44
Maybe God Invented Hot Flashes	45
Prayer on the Morning of My Fiftieth Birthday	47

III

Show and Tell	51
How to Get to Heaven	52
The Captured Angel Comments on Communion	54
The Back of Christ	55
Trying to Name It	57
Teresa's World	59
The Only Thing I Ever Stole	61
What the Leaves Said	63
Cancer Clinic	64
The Captured Angel Sings a Psalm of Beholding	66
Noumenon	68
Theophany	69

IV

Tips from an Ant	73
The Captured Angel Comments on Boredom	74
On This Earth	75
Drowning My Sorrows	77
Blind Hopes	79
On a Weekend Visit, I Drink My Coffee	81
The Last Leaf	83
Space	84
Hearing	85
Feeding My Mother Jell-O in the Hospital	87
The Death Catcher	88
Eternity	89
The Captured Angel Comments on My Future Self	90
Dear Specter, One More Thing	91

Acknowledgments	93
About the Author	95

*When I consider the brief span of my life—the small
space I occupy and which I see swallowed up in the
infinite immensity of spaces of which I know nothing—
I am amazed to see myself here rather than there...
now rather than then. Who put me here?
By whose command and act were this place
and time allotted to me?*

—Pascal

I

Owner's Manual

In the womb I was given
the owner's manual
for my life.

I left it inside my mother.

Often I dream I've shrunk
myself down,
with a tiny flashlight
entered the deep-dark cave.

Finally I find it. On
page one something like:
How to Translate the Wind's Gibberish.
On page two: How to Make Wine
from Suffering's Grapes.

Once I couldn't locate
the exit,
considered growing
my way out
but that would have burst my mother.
Then I woke.

I always forget what
the manual says.
Only once was I able
to scribble some words
and bring them back:

Love the rose because it will soon be gone.
Learn to walk as if your feet are kissing the earth.

The Captured Angel Confesses

Okay, okay, I confess the boss said
to give you ripe melons, cool beakers

of wine, sunsets, kisses, each other's flesh
to lick and nibble but also

the time bomb no one sees or hears
ticking, planted somewhere

beneath your ribs. And in the cavern
of your mother's womb when you asked

for a flashlight, it was me
that pushed the pen into your tiny hand,

me that told you to just hurry—sign
on the dotted line without reading

the fine print. I extracted
memory. You hardly felt it.

Sorry for lust. Obviously
I poured too much into that teeny

test tube between your legs.
And neurotic tendencies? My bad.

Intricate wiring's not my strength.
Yes, I cut corners. A slight slipup

with that temper of yours. It's no picnic
being cramped in an oozy bubble

all those months. You had to grow
but I had to work with such small tools.

Torture all you want, I won't reveal
the expiration date stamped

on your forehead. I got some things right.
Who do you think untangled the slippery cord

from around your neck? Who do you think
picked for you such good parents?

Sixth Birthday: The Transparent Model Man

Six-year-olds shouldn't know
the brain is spaghetti and the cranium
is the bowl. Or that the heart is not
a doily-trimmed valentine.
Or under every smile and frown
the skull's poker face waits.
They shouldn't know eyeballs
without eyelids never blink—
that we all stare like zombies.
That the body is nothing more
than plumbing—valves clog,
pipes burst. They shouldn't know
it can happen mid-slurp eating soup,
the spoon an inch from lips.
Inner coils can pop. They might start
to see in slow motion
and in reverse. It will be a blessing
and a curse. How do you make
a poet, or at least a man in love
with death? Show the boy
how skin is a sack
holding us in. That without bones
we'd be puddles. That rivers
of blood wait to spill out.

The Secret Power

My father used to reupholster
  people, stitching them back
    together like torn pillows

made new. He earned a living
  holding lungs
    like water balloons,

cutting them open
  to find mushrooming
    tumors. He strummed

ribs, watched the heart
  like a chick in a shell
    spasm, quiver.

As a kid, knowing this,
  I developed x-ray vision,
    could see through everyone

like a window, or more like
  a fish tank, all their stuffing
    swimming inside them.

How alike we are,
  I kept discovering:
    pancreas, liver, intestines,

all in the same spots,
  same colors
    and shapes, not to mention

chunks of food in every
   stomach sloshing.
      In school I'd sit distracted,

watching kids' digestive
   juices emulsifying
      their lunches, nibble

my sandwich, look down
   at my own belly. As
      an adult I've held

women in my arms,
   made love and seen
      without the fancy

wrapping despite what we
   call lust or fear of
      separation, inside

gears and whirligigs
   spinning. I've raised
      two children, known

they are smaller models
   of the same bloody
      contraption; one day

a bolt comes loose,
   a wire short-circuits,
      the inner factory

shuts down production.
   I lie in bed
      with my wife,

her thigh draped
   across my waist,
     her head

on my shoulder,
   air sifting in and out
     of nostrils. I see

her lungs inflate,
   deflate over and over.
     In the dark, I think back

to my father, how he'd come
   home not knowing
     he'd given his son

a secret power,
   how he'd ask about
     my day, not sharing

his, of all the bodies
   fixed and some beyond
     repair. I'd tell him

I got an A or how at recess
   I hit the winning homer,
     he'd hug me then change

clothes, then lie on the couch
   as I watched him doze,
     as I tried to locate

the thing we call love
   like an exotic, bright fish
     never really spotted

swimming inside us.
  I kiss my wife's forehead,
    before I close my eyes

take one last peek at
  the beautiful, strange cauliflower
    inside her skull's cave.

Early Lesson

When I saw the amputee
I thought she was dying in pieces.

She was the lady
behind the counter using one arm

to work the register. I wondered if next
her other arm would fall off

like an apple from a branch,
ripe and heavy, or if

a leg or ear or maybe her nose
would drop right in front of us,

my mother and me, any second.
That night I couldn't sleep,

kept wondering when my pieces
would start falling like flower petals,

imagined walking to school
leaving a trail of fingers, toes,

arms, legs, lying
on the sidewalk unable to go

farther, a torso and head,
then the torso gone, finally

just my head, flies nesting
in nostrils, a group of boys

deciding to play soccer telling me
to shut up every time they kicked

and I screamed. Was a new
disease spreading?

I started to notice
people every day missing parts—

bus driver with an eye patch,
TV repairman minus fingers,

man with no legs on a piece of wood
wheeling through the alley.

I pictured a lost-and-found heaven
of piled-up human scraps, but how

would we ever find our pieces
among the millions, the ones that matched,

fit and clicked back into place?
Finally I asked Mother

who only said those people had accidents,
that's why she always scolded

Be careful. But I knew none of us
were put together very well, I knew

this whole living thing
was just a matter of time.

Spirits

I asked about the word
on the store window,
so when my uncle pulled me in
holding his big hand,

I thought all the bottles
on the shelves held
dead people's souls.
I'd heard of genies in lamps,

seen cartoons, how puffs
of ghost squirt out and float.
When he bought a jug
he said was Bourbon,

good for toothaches, I thought
the dead man's name was Bourbon,
a dentist before he croaked.
It sat between us in the front

all the drive back to my folks
where lots of other grown-ups
nibbled snacks and scooped ice
from a silver bucket.

Music played, the grown-ups
seemed happy, talking loud.
Mother made me a sandwich
with fancy crustless bread,

sent me to bed with a kiss.
I wondered all night
what happened when Bourbon
was released. Would he find me,

slink under the door? And how
many other spirits swirled,
all those open bottles
on the kitchen table?

When Mother popped
her head in to say goodnight,
I couldn't speak, just let her
peck my cheek and turn off

the light. Through the door
I heard singing, laughter,
ice cubes clinking glass,
pictured milky splashes

of light above grown-ups' heads,
looking down, telling jokes about
being alive once. Maybe they dove
into some of the bodies, dipped

through flesh to feel it briefly
again. Come morn I couldn't
eat my cornflakes, kept scanning
the ceiling, for years after swore

I was being watched from every
corner. Why would grown-ups
invite dead people to a party?
I never asked. But sometimes,

even now, dozing off, empty
tumbler beside me, I'll jerk
awake, something corkscrewing
its way through my chest.

Sweetness

Standing next to me in the pew
he slipped me a candy root beer barrel
to suck during the dull sermon,
as if to say thinking about
God doesn't require a lack
of all pleasure. Then before the priest
finished his endless ranting on heaven
and hell, my father sneaked us out
the small side door marked
Emergency Exit,

which this was. He drove us
to Mister Donut for cream sticks and cocoa
while everyone else sat sweating
in the cramped church,
force-fed God-this, God-that.

What we talked about I don't remember,
but it wasn't sin or damnation,
and instead of a cube of bread and sip
of wine we gulped maple icing,
doughy pastry, washed down with
liquid chocolate, our communion.

Then he offered me Bazooka bubble gum,
pink corn syrup and sugar congealed—
to clear the palate, he said—
as if to hammer home that God dwells
in sweetness and more sweetness
in the least likely of places,

even a greasy donut shop
where a father and son hunch,
shoulder to shoulder,
at a chipped plastic counter.

Death and Birth

Men give birth. I've seen it.
When my father gave birth to his death
it filled the room with heaving sobs.
It threw things and shook the walls.
It was too wild for the hospital halls,
so we took it home but it was too wild
for the house. In a matter of days
it even poked its head
through clouds. How adorable!

It has calmed down
but needs to stop
sucking its thumb.

When I give birth to my death
I hope it grows big and strong.
Boy or girl doesn't matter,
as long as it's healthy
and lives a long, happy life.

Siste Viator

The inscription on Roman roadside tombs,
meaning, *Stop Traveler*, as if the dead want
the living to pause for a cup of tea,
a chat about what it's like being dead.
Of course, I stop, can hear them
snickering, *What a sucker*, in Italian.
But they must secretly love how
I bend forward on one knee,
my face inches from the stone
trying to make out the small carved
message, thinking of my friend
George who hanged himself in jail
with his belt after being caught stealing
steaks from the grocery where he worked;
and Paul with AIDS lying in the hospital
the day before stepping off the planet,
murmuring his regret at never having
made love to a man who couldn't
speak English; and my father,
seeing again his shinbone poking
through skin, the compound fracture
that led to the infection that led to
the sudden coma that led to the
dying. How he was playing in the yard
with my daughter—
slipped, fell oddly.
How I thought his squeals
were mischief, part of the game. How
as they wheeled him into Emergency
telling him it was just a bad break,
he said he knew he wouldn't be coming
back home, as if God or the devil

had whispered into his ear.
The dead Italians must enjoy the flood
of memories when someone stops,
looking at the stone, which for them
is a window—their faces pressed eagerly
to the glass, inches from our faces
their heads tilted, ears cupped by a hand
to hear more distinctly our thoughts.

My Father's Death Turns One Year Old

I threw him a party.
We sat together on a chair.
He was old enough now to know how he was born.
I told him.
He wanted to see the photo.
I showed him your face.
We could both see the resemblance.
He asked what he'll become.
I said there is no word for it.
Then we had some cake and several glasses of bourbon,
which made us groggy, so we fell asleep on the chair.

The Sweat Mark

The face on his t-shirt
after the run
was his father's,
no doubt:
Greek eyes, high cheekbones,
dimpled chin—no mistaking,
as he stood
before the mirror,
running fingers through his own
slick hair.
He'd had sweat marks before,
but never this:
eyebrows, nostrils,
crooked smirk—
wistful, wise.
Should he save it
like a relic, take
a photo to prove the magic?
Too late. The face changed
into a goat, then a tree, drying up.
Then just a blank canvas
in front of glass
where he chilled,
so he stripped,
looked up at his own face
then down to the shed mask
on floor tiles,
and there—
his dead father's creased forehead

he should have kissed
in the hospital
those final moments
but didn't.

The Captured Angel Comments on Death

It's a great invention.
People are a lot nicer
when they're dead.
They don't get impatient
waiting in line at the license bureau.
They don't turn red
and flip you the finger
in traffic and they don't tear
pages out of magazines in
waiting rooms.
They don't fart in elevators or
fake orgasms.
You can say whatever you want
and they won't fire back a sarcastic remark;
in fact, they are great listeners
and will not squirm or rush you
through the boring account
of your day. They don't invent
interrogation devices to electrocute
your genitals. They don't place X's
on a map where bombs will be dropped.
They don't make speeches sprinkled
with promises they'll never keep.
They are much like old furniture
sitting silently, unthreatening,
docile, stored in an attic—
or like an imaginary friend from
childhood you could tell
anything to and boss around.
And best of all about the dead
is you don't have to wonder

if they really love you or are being dutiful
or if they still think sadly
about that time after the spat
when you said
you wished they were dead.

II

While You Were Gone Getting Tomatoes for Our Salad

I telepathically spoke to the head of lettuce.
I inquired about greenness.
I riffed on salad art and spinach-envy.
I tried to cheer him up.
Picture, I said, starving children in India,
their bones screaming through skin;
what they wouldn't do for a leaf of you now,
I told him. How important you are
in this big crazy world.
Not to mention all those vitamins you carry
like so many credit cards.
But the lettuce was depressed.
Nothing seemed to work.
So I entertained him
with how I stomped grapes
with bare feet, I described
the honey-wheat smell
of my daughter's hair.
I told him how I chased seagulls on a beach
with my son in Cozumel.
I mentioned the highway
between your nipple and neck,
the rest stop of your collarbone,
how you always step out of jeans, dainty,
like you're climbing a barbed-wire fence.
Which backfired.
He saw how much better it is to be human.
But I felt happier.
Then you came home and we put the lettuce
out of his misery.

Upon Discovering My Daughter's Tattoo

                Some sort of Indian flower,
she will explain,
on her right hip
above the globe where ass flattens
into spine,
                but I am still in the gap
between the second I spot it
as she leans forward on the futon
and her shirt rises
and the second I will say,
                "So, you got one,"
pointing. In the millisecond I press *pause*
on the remote in my chest
freezing my daughter as she reaches
for the fallen potato chip
so I can examine the tattoo more closely
without rushing.
                I zoom in,
my face almost touching her skin,
eyeballing ornate petals and the stem
she will tell me is a Hindu
umbilical cord connecting
the beautiful blossom
to the earth it sprung from,
and the thought that I am that soil
and she is that flower
will rise in my skull
and the stem that connects us
is all the moments between
when she popped into the world
and right now.

                I get up, walk around, look
into her dazzling mocha eyes, unblinking,
her mouth in mid-smile, the teeth
straight and white,
her slender arm extended,
the fingers of her hand reaching for
the chip on the floor.
                I stroke her silky
hair, place
a strand that flung itself
over her eyes
behind her ear.
I whisper you will always be
my little blossom
no matter what you do to the canvas
of your body, or where you go
and with or without whom,
that ancient father rebel cry of love.
                I sit back on the futon,
almost ready,
wondering if she'll notice her hair
magically readjusted as she scoops
the chip. I breathe in deep,
look at the flower, quite delicate,
one more time,
exhale,
press *play* on my remote.

The Artist

My little son draws an ocean and above it
prehistoric-looking birds.
A ship with stick figure men in hats
on deck. A sun with lines
of heat spoking out.

There is a small clump of land,
an island, and on it a single
palm tree. He adds one,
then a second coconut
which has fallen on sand.

Now nineteen he sits
beside me in the car,
staring out the window while we drive
to college. He wants to be an actor
but he can't see

behind my forehead
into my skull's theater
the big screen where he stars,
a six-year-old hunched at the table
with a father recently divorced

who writes checks paying bills
as snow piles up and wind howls
rattling windows,
the father daydreaming
a tropical paradise

with umbrella drinks
and brown-skinned goddesses,
place of no guilt
for once, another Paul Gaugin.
Then the little son adds

a stick figure man and stick figure
boy next to the coconuts,
gives the father the sketch
and says,
"I took us on vacation."

I turn the radio up, then tap his knee
and he turns to me, surprised. We
just look at each other a moment,
keep driving past farm houses,
billboards, oceans of wheat.

I Drive Through a Blizzard for a Cup of Tea

I don't even like tea. Piss water with lemon.
But my son has invited me. This boy
I thought I'd lost and would never see again.
Our tents near a lake, dusk falling. His mother
cleaning dishes, me helping a fellow
camper pump his tires. Then blackness.
Where is he? Age four, did he wander off?
Was he snatched by some pervert?
Dear God in heaven. This boy.
Is he in someone's tent begging
not to be touched? Is he in someone's car
heading to a seedy motel or dark alley?
Is he face-down, bobbing in the lake?
I run barefoot for miles, screaming:
Where are you Jonathan? Where are you,
son? Minutes like hours. Making deals
with God. Then finally, a park ranger
finds him a block away at the playground
swinging all alone. "I just wanted fun,
Daddy."

Through sheets of white.
Sub-zero temps.
Sliding, barely avoiding a ditch.
I arrive.
He greets me.
We sit on his couch.
He tells me about his first role,
Shakespeare's Tybalt.
This boy I almost lost forever.

Then he explains the benefits
of green tea. Antioxidants.
How it makes you more alive.
We part the curtains and watch the snow.
He brings out his costume.
We joke about the tights. This boy.
I sip the pale green liquid,
finish, ask for more.

Miscarriage

At Starbuck's
my daughter tells me.

No words volunteer
to rise through my throat's

tunnel to sacrifice themselves—
cowards.

So I catch one of her
teardrops, peel away

the outer layer, pin back
the glistening skin.

Inside I find a control room,
like a cockpit of a craft.

The pilot must have seen me
coming, must have vaporized

himself to avoid interrogation.
We are not meant to know

the secret mission of whoever
trains them, little kamikazes

studying maps of where
they will fall (what it must be

like to navigate, looking out
transparent walls).

Across the silence
like a vast tundra

I watch her eyes—
more tearnauts tumble

down her cheeks.
On her bagel

the shattered liquid
spaceships spell something

invisible. I think
it says, *Hold me. Daddy,*

just hold me.

Kitchen Jeopardy

When I hang-up the phone after the telemarketer says
he sincerely cares about my future,

the captured angel becomes Alex Trebec
between the sink and microwave.

He announces the next category: *What People Really Mean
When They Say Things*. "I'll take the category for $100, Alex."

"*Have a nice day at the cashier's check-out*." "What is:
I guess I'd hope you have a better day than a bad one,

but I really don't care." "Correct, you control the board."
"Same category for $200, Alex." "*Hello, how are you*

in the hallway at work." "What is: I confirm your bodily
presence but am not interested and hope you just

say *fine*, which could mean wonderful or awful,
heartbroken or inspired, instead of making me pause

to hear about your flat tire or paper cut." "Correct again."
"*What People Really Mean* for $300."

"*Going through some things*." "What is: a sex life
on the rocks or renewed addiction." "Yes, you got it!"

"*What People Really Mean* for $400." "*It's God's will*."
"What is: I can't fathom the meaningless absurdity,

randomness and horror of existence without pretending
it all makes sense." "Bravo. Right again."

"*What People Really Mean* for $500." "It's the Daily Double!
What's your wager?" "I'll bet it all, Alex." "OK, here it is:

*I love you before your children hang up the phone
500 miles away.*" "What is: We understand why you split

our hearts in two, why in each half you installed a revolving
door, why you taught us a new vocabulary including

shared parenting, child support, visitation schedule,
why you made us sometimes feel like turtles ripped

from their shells; we forgive you the emotional baggage
you made us pack and lug back and forth between houses,

we forgive the awkward silences, how you always got smaller
as we pulled away up the street looking back at you

waving goodbye in the driveway." "Oh…I am sorry. So close.
The answer is, What is: *We are still trying to understand—*

and so on, and *we hope to someday forgive you—*
I nod, then take out all the *I love yous*

I've saved since the beginning, stacked in piles in my skull—
always room for more, each slightly different, like a fossil

or rare coin. I finger them, hold them up to the light,
tilt them this way and that, show them off.

Alex leans against the fridge, says "Very nice, but
we must move on."

I carefully put them back. "Yes, yes," I say.
Alex announces the next category.

The Captured Angel Comments on Blame

Don't blame
the failure of the floor
to speak
of your bare feet.

Don't blame
the failure of
the block of space
called a room
to explain
how it feels when
you walk through it.

Don't blame
the failure of walls
to tell the story of
your shadow

or the failure of,
especially,
the bed,
to describe the ache
of withdrawal
when you're not in it.

Blame your ears
you never upgraded.
Blame your eyes.

How many hours
of silence
have you filled
with noise?
How many times
have you rushed
past a tree
bending its branches
in deference

to something
of which it knows
nothing,
and didn't notice?

As the Gods Booby-Trap Love

The Inuit hunters admire the bear.
They would never call it stupid or reckless,
though it might be.
They are in awe of its hunger.
They believe the bear knows the sharpened
wolf bone is buried in the blubber
and that somewhere in its primitive brain
the bear glimpses the terrible tearing apart
that will occur: the trail of blood
over miles, days, the crucifixion
from inside-out. They consider
the mutilated bear heroic,
believe the beast chooses the temporary
miracle of the rigged meal,
its sweet juices, one-of-a-kind flavor,
knowingly and regardless.

In Praise of Surrealism

Since the mind loves its cotton candy electrocuted.

Since the skull's living room needs furniture rearranged
now and then to keep things fresh.

Since I enjoy watching my snores line up to reenter my mouth.

Since through every object's keyhole I peep.

Since you haven't lived until you've witnessed zeroes
gather on a hill and start to bleat.

Since a billion trillion years from now exists.
And the air held together with pins.
And the tendons beneath my lover's knees
stitched to my forehead.

Since fireflies in the yard are angels with glowing erections
or souls arriving and departing in collision-creating sparks.

Since I can wring out an icicle with my bare hands if I want to.

Since raindrops clinging to branches are waterberries I pluck
and take home to bake delicious waterberry pie.

Since I know a bone caught in the wind's throat when I hear it.

Since there are not enough drugs in the universe for me
to ever see God's face.

In Praise of the Ordinary

When you're with me you kick surrealism out of the house.

                How nice of you. Please stay.

      Let it rearrange somebody else's furniture, you say, things as they are can be enough.

                You present the evidence:

    hollows of your collarbones
    where water collects

               when you step from the shower,

    twisted vines of hair,
    corded neck,
            elegant throat,

each lax muscle of your naked flesh,

pelvic curve as you lie on your side,

    and the smallest blue veins

              on the back of one of your hands.

Maybe God Invented Hot Flashes

        to see if the husband will
softly blow cool breezes from his mouth
onto his wife's flushed neck.
Or better yet,
to see if he reaches
across erupting volcanoes
of her heaving breasts
to the small bedside fan
aimed at her face,
flicking the *On* button
to jet-stream level
his mouth can't match.
Or better still,
to see if he might throw off
comfy covers and stumble naked
through the dark,
down stairs, returning with an ice cube
like a sacred offering
he places on the altar of her forehead.

        Maybe God invented hot flashes
to witness what happens more often—
the woman huffing, waking
the man, and she rolls away
from him creating
the widest possible space.
To spy the man who knows the drill
and rolls the other way
to the farthest edge of the mattress,
mumbles, "Do you need anything?"
and she snaps, "Don't dare touch me."
And when the smoldering coal of her body

finally, blessedly cools,
she reaches across the bed's empty canyon
as if to say it's ok, I'm back, I'm yours,
weaves her fingers with the man's
and they fall asleep again holding hands.

Prayer on the Morning of My Fiftieth Birthday

Dear specter
with a thousand faces
changing like a hologram
of every salesman I've ever known
or will know
who visited me last night in my dream
to say: *Happy fiftieth,*
I'll take muscle tone from your arms,
your perpetual erections,
your incredible tolerance for spicy Mexican food,
but the rest of you can stay—

thank you
for the bargain—

cool air through vents above my bed,
a woman's blond hair splayed
across the pillow,
slight ache in my knee
adding just a twinge to foreground
the perfection as sun through blinds
stripes the wall and under crisp-clean sheets
her thigh, her one and only dewy smell.

III

Show and Tell

At a roadside stand in Kentucky,
a porous plastic figurine
with instructions at the base:

Pour beet juice in Christ and watch him bleed.

I bought it in case one day I'm asked
to present to another-world alien
an artifact of my people.

He will know what we're like—

evolved, inventive, spiritual.

He might give it to his little son or daughter
who might take it to school for show and tell,
the way I took a statue of Achilles,
souvenir from Greece.

All the other little aliens will *ooh* and *aah*
and the teacher with three heads will pull down
a map of the universe on the wall,
pointing to our planet trying to explain
about the invention of gods

as a curious little critter in the back raises her claw
wanting to know what beet juice is,
and why there are holes.

How to Get to Heaven

In the restroom, strategically placed,
on top of the urinal,
one of those religious pamphlets
titled *How to Get to Heaven*.
Someone knew there'd be no choice
but to stare at the cover:
a man with a confused look
kneeling between God and the Devil.
The man is trying to decide
who to follow—

the Devil dressed in black
holding what looks like a bottle
of top-shelf scotch in one hand
and in the other a thick wad of
dollar bills as behind him
a beautiful naked woman,
his assistant, I assume, stands
with long hair and horns
seductively winking—
or God, who has a beard,
a bible tucked under one arm,
a staff He leans on, and sandals.
Below the picture, we are told,
the outcome of choosing the Devil
is on page one, the outcome
of choosing God on page five.
But we know how it ends, we all do.
Booze and money and women
with horns are bad, an old hippie
with a beard and a bible is good.

I zip up, can't resist.
On page one the man is drowning
in an ocean of flames.
On page five he reclines on a cloud
as if it's a hammock.
Pages two, three, and four instruct
how to get to that perfect sky-pillow:
the man praying in a church,
helping an old lady cross the street,
reading to a sick boy in a hospital.
But what if the scotch mellows
the man, puts him in a praying mood?
What if he uses the money to give
to the poor? What if loving the horny
woman gets him in touch with
a deeper, spiritual side, teaches
tenderness and, when she leaves him
for somebody else, instructs how
to let go of pleasure and need
through something called pain?
Page six says the choice is mine.
I leave the pamphlet for the next guy.
Wash my hands. Go back to my stool
at the bar. Order a double.

The Captured Angel Comments on Communion

Have you spoken to a crumb?
Have you lowered your head,
crumb-level, whispered:
Please let me in?
Have you told it the pleasures
of eating and sleeping,
what it's like to grow old
and think about death?
Have you apologized for
having said more than once
in your life, "I feel crummy"?
Have you asked if it has nightmares
about ants? Have you held it
on your palm like a diamond?
Have you knocked on its
white door? Have you considered
all the crumbs that have
tumbled from lips since
the beginning? Have you
placed it on your tongue
giving thanks for the thing
itself and what it stands for?

The Back of Christ

> *Three men broke into his New York studio while the Spanish Pavilion displayed the painting "The Back of Christ" at the 1964 World's Fair in New York. They crushed his hands. Thomas Fundora was not able to paint for nine years.*
> —The Miami Herald, August 28, 1998

Because no Christ should lack a face, they said.

Because He's turned away from us.

Because Jesus would at least glance back.

Because it terrifies, a God so anonymous.

Because He prefers to look ahead.

Because we'll never catch up.

Because a rear view is a sign of disrespect.

Because we feel left out.

Because He could be smiling or frowning, He could be rolling His eyes in disgust.

Because He doesn't appear to be showing the way, just standing.

Because God is never just standing.

Because the back of His head is a mask.

Because from this angle He's a closed door.

Because God would never shut us out.

Because our birthright is to know.

Because the hard work of following is hard.

Because that could be anyone with long hair.

Because God speaks through an artist's hands and God would never say this.

Because mashing knuckles with a hammer
was a kind of prayer.

Because screams bouncing off walls was like a choir.

Because tough love was called for.

Because religion.

Because He died for us.

Because the blood, the men are quoted as saying,
was the real painting God intended.

And it was everywhere.

Trying to Name It

There's something about Max,
the short pudgy guy who delivers
papers. It's not the fact
that in his thirties he has
an eight- or nine-year-old brain.
Nor that every afternoon he pedals
his sky blue Schwinn with a basket
that holds the rolled-up news of this
world. It's not how when he arrives
at my mailbox and sees me on my porch
he smiles, waves, yells,
"Here's your paper, Mr. Neil!"
It's not his t-shirt always sweat-soaked, sticking
to rolls of fat around his middle.
Not his thick fingers that once handed
me the paper through my open car window,
which must have been a stroke of luck
because he said, "Aren't we lucky,"
then giggled.
It's not his one crooked eye permanently gazing
up and to the left as if it scans
for something outside the scene
no one else can see.
Not his missing front tooth,
the gap that causes him to spray
when he talks, especially if he's excited.
It's not the way he stops pedaling
when a neighbor's black Lab runs up
and he straddles the bike in the middle
of the street stroking the dog's head,
letting the dog lick his news-ink stained hands.

No. It has more to do with how
if you stood beside me on the grass—
I invite you, stand beside me—
you too would hear him telling the dog
something private, in whispers, like a secret
as we strain to make out words,
the dog resting its chin so calmly
on Max's knee. How looking up into
the pasty face
which Max has lowered so they are nearly
nose to nose, the animal doesn't blink,
and we watch in wonder
like some cave man or woman looking up
at Sirius, the Dog Star, the brightest,
before things had names,
as he kisses the furry black noggin
three times—a sort of prayer—
then pedals off down the street.

Teresa's World

The neighbor girl, third grade,
made it with her father.
A school project—they carved
entire mountain ranges
out of styrofoam blocks,
crinkled foil to be an ocean,
glued sand for a beach.
They created a jungle from grass
and snips of the backyard pine's
prickly branches.
One day they saw me
walking, invited me in,
so proud to show
the tiny plastic townspeople
boarding a train, marching into
a church, playing on a miniature
playground. There was a farm
with little cows and pigs,
a windmill with twirling blades.
I remember how
the little girl said it took
four whole weeks to build,
almost a year ago. Now
a month since the drowning
I watch from my porch
her father, who could be a god,
drag it out of the garage
to the yard, where
with newspapers and twigs,

he makes a small fire
then stands a long time
studying the flames,
letting it all vanish.

The Only Thing I Ever Stole

A rock.
But not just any.
I was ten,
in Athens,
with my parents.
DO NOT TOUCH. DO NOT TAKE.
REMOVAL OF ROCKS PUNISHABLE BY LAW.
Signs all over the Parthenon.

I bent down to tie my shoe, pretending,
slipped one into my pocket.
I carried it, sweating,
past guards, tour guides,
fingering its smooth marble,
praying. On the flight home,
thirteen hours, I did the same,
eyeing stewardesses who were
undercover FBI.

And here it sits on my desk,
40 years later. Here I still see
Socrates, Plato, sandaled, stepping
on it, Alexander the Great
rubbing it for luck.
I wanted the eternal, the unchanging.
Or as close as I could get.
Something that's witnessed
continents splitting, melting,
milk in glass bottles,
Hitler.

The world becomes more mysterious,
not less, the more we know—
the rock doesn't say this.
The rock's lips are sealed.
On my desk beside computer, phone,
its silence mocks them.
How hard they try, straining.
Oh, poor little gadgets gadgeting.
(I read the rock's mind,
the rock inscrutably at peace with itself).
Poor man, hair whitening, skin slackening.
Poor world.
Poor, poor delicate things
in such a hurry.

What the Leaves Said

That they don't do birthdays or have funerals.
That the wind has mood swings even they can't predict.
That the possibility the wind is God is too obvious to discuss.
That the roots of the tree sometimes speak to them in dreams.
That they have never witnessed a mosquito begging
to be forgiven.
That they admire the tight-lipped stones.
That letting go is not a choice.
That the evergreens are boring and self-righteous.
That the only things on Earth smarter than them
are ocean waves.
That squirrel feet tickle.
That raindrops are snacks.
That no leaf is lunatic enough to pick itself up and try
to reattach to the branch.
That in the dark they still watch us.
That being naked is nice.
That they are not ashamed to dance with many partners.
That they know how lucky they are to be here a short time
to listen to the birds,
to notice a cat curled on a porch,
to blow kisses to the garbage men clanking cans at 5 a.m.,
to listen to the crickets.

Cancer Clinic

I was running oh so late,
couldn't find the new office
my dentist had moved to,
I was cursing the secretary
who had given me instructions,
cursing slow cars and red lights,
cursing the whole goddamn universe,
slapping the steering wheel
when I screeched into a lot,
jumped from my car
into a building
to ask directions,
and who would have thought
you could step onto another planet
so easily, where aliens
looked like skeletons
in skull caps,
some in wheelchairs,
most with bulging eyes,
long bony fingers turning pages,
a little girl creature
being helped toward an open door
by two human-looking women
dressed in white, one on each side
holding a twig-like arm,
all three of them smiling,
the girl-thing staring down at her feet
the way a baby does
learning to walk, tiny steps,
and there was no impatience or anger

even though the door held open
by a human-looking man also in white
must have seemed a mile away
as they scuffed forward
across the planet's linoleum surface
reminding me of turtles,
the way I'd watch them as a boy
near a pond, afternoons in summer,
sun on my face,
fishing pole in one hand
sandwich in the other,
back on my planet,
and it didn't matter
where I was from
or where I was going—
I couldn't remember any more—
as I stood staring
until they made their way,
reached the door,
and passed through.

The Captured Angel Sings a Psalm of Beholding

Behold the sun spitting oranges.
Behold the news carried by each drop of rain.

Behold the tire swing lonelier than any god, not swinging.
Behold the bird that thinks an airplane is God.

Behold the leaf committing suicide tired of being a leaf.
Behold the sad moth trying to break into a light bulb
    to fry himself on the wires.

Behold steaks in the freezer dreaming of the Almighty Cow.
Behold frozen peas that sound like glass tears
    when they hit the plate.

Behold chalk that knows how erasure tastes.
Behold every color being born waving goodbye to its white.

Behold the wind with a hard-on trying to undress the trees.
Behold air's parentheses around every object.

Behold matches sleeping together in a box.
Behold the pencil in the mug that remembers once being sharp.

Behold moondust through the window on the floor
    spelling a name.
Behold the face behind a thumbnail looking up at a girl
    spreading polish with a brush.

Behold coins in a pocket in love with distant *chinks*
    of someone playing horseshoes.
Behold two children arguing in a sandbox:
    "It's a desert." "No, It's a beach."

Behold the wasted day hoping to be invited back.
Behold the white streams of two planes, a cross fading.

Behold the lipstick kiss on a glass's rim.
Behold kneecap-toenail-instep erotic metaphysics.

Behold the bald child playing jacks on the stoop of the wig shop.
Behold the prosthetic of her hope that lets her hobble along.

Behold the scarecrow crucified in corn.
Behold his enormous straw head bending as if he's praying.

Behold imagination holding up a sign: WILL WORK FOR FOOD.
Behold people rushing past it to houses where TVs grow fat.

Behold the school vomiting teenagers.
Behold the cell phone sucking brains through a man's ear.

Behold the sacredness of that moth's dusty wings before he dies.
Behold the quiet sermon of crickets that speak of
    your life's ten million choices.

Behold two crows facing off, between them pizza crust
    left in a box.
Behold history with its yellow teeth and bad breath.

Behold the vase full of flowers that won't be coming back.
Behold the piñata of any moment, this brief being here
    to smash it open.

Noumenon

As for the woman digging in a dumpster, pulling out banana peels, empty cans, an old sneaker, twisted hangers, newspapers, and then a plastic Christ pinned to a white cross looking up as if to heaven pleading to be saved, as the story goes, now smeared with tomato sauce and coffee grounds—I will not say she was an angel in disguise. I will not claim I saw with x-ray eyes through gnarled clothes and pocked skin to something glowing the way a light bulb does when covered by a towel. For all I know she could have been a wrecking ball to the glass house of a child's heart, as far from any god as you or me. I will not make more of her and what I witnessed than what it was: how she held the startled Christ up to get a better look. How beside the Walmart she started to laugh at a thought or memory no one could see, then noticed me watching as I loaded my car with bags of food—and like a deer in the headlights froze, then kept on digging.

Theophany

A little boy is flying a kite in the park.
You ask if he tied the handkerchief
to the tail for balance.
He looks in your eyes, quite serious, says
no, it is to dry the tears
of the clouds up there.
Then he hands you the string
and says, here you try,
it's not so hard.
And together you both watch
the kite dip and soar,
up and down, back and forth,
doing the impossible
for all of us.

IV

Tips from an Ant

Beware the other-side-of–the-tracks colony,
the sniffing ant-sucking dog.
Watch where you walk:
tree sap-quick sand,
the open book snapping shut.
Beware of boys with firecrackers
and magnifying glasses.
If it looks too good to be true—
whole slice of pizza on cement—
it probably is.
No such thing as a free lunch,
or picnic for that matter.
Never take off your helmet.
Give thanks for each crumb.
Now and then look up:
blue sky glimpse of what
was here before you.
Brass knuckles and switchblades
don't work. Keep loving the world.
As a last resort play dead
and think like a pebble.

The Captured Angel Comments on Boredom

Some people are boring because their parents had
boring sex the night they were conceived.
Which spreads boredom everywhere. And isn't their fault.

But most of you fall out of love with amazement.
With the way hummingbird wings sound like questions.
With how a rotted mango left out turns into a perfect

sitting room for wasps. With a creature like the cuttlefish
that when starving will eat its own heart. With a stone frog
in a garden and on its head a butterfly with sore feet.

With how electric bug zappers on porches at night set free
tiny spirits and fireflies in yards could be dead people
lighting cigarettes. With how birds doze on wires perfectly still—

without waking in mid-air, tumbling terrified from nightmares.
Yes, some people are boring because they were the spark when
two boring people rubbed their genitals together like sticks.

Which spreads the disease. But most of you fall out of love
with the rich broth of dusk. With the way sky is daily washed by
the rough nurse of morning. With silence in a room

that is the opposite of nails being pounded in a roof.
With how any given moment, you can spot a child tugging
a grown-up's hand, giggling, pointing at things that she wants.

On This Earth

     My friend was late,
so in the coffee shop
   I watched a little girl
so excited by her cookie
    on the plate

    that she giggled
and clapped her hands
   and looked up at
her father with wide eyes
    then back down

    at her cookie,
which was yellow
   with a black icing eye
to resemble a bird.
    She touched it

    with her finger,
smiled a missing tooth
   smile, gazed up again
at her father
    who also smiled,

    and she giggled some more.
Which is when
   my friend arrived
and I said thanks
    for being late,

    which I meant
but he took
    as sarcasm, as the father
opened a newspaper
    full of things that had

    already happened
and the girl—
    though I don't know
what words can do
    to honor what I saw—

    in the perfect bubble
of the present moment
    took a nibble
and started to wiggle
    on her chair.

Drowning My Sorrows

I try to drown my sorrows
but my sorrows can swim.
They backstroke, splash
in a pond of tequila.
So I make a lake
of bourbon. They laugh,
play Marco Polo. Next,
an ocean of vodka.
They float on their backs.
Oh, I know my sorrows
are little sorrows
compared to the horrors on TV.
But damn, they're resourceful.
Some use ice cubes as rafts.
They even work together,
bigger ones hoisting
smaller ones on their shoulders.
I look down into the glass:
my father's last words,
my neighbor's face
after his grandson blew up
in Iraq, my widow mother
alone in her house
talking to photos;
and, of course, scars
from my divorce,
little life preservers other sorrows
cling to (What have I done?
Oh, my poor children).
I add rum, gin,

tidal waves, tsunamis.
Pour some wine,
no ice cubes this time.
They vanish and for awhile
I can breathe.
They hold their breath.
Their tiny heads bob
like buoyant corks,
mouths agape.

Blind Hopes

Chorus: Did you perhaps go further than you have told us?
Prometheus: I caused mortals to cease foreseeing doom.
Chorus: What cure did you provide them against that sickness?
Prometheus: I placed in them blind hopes.
　　　　　　　—Aeschylus

They can't see a damn thing,
I love them anyway.
They tap their white canes,
sometimes still bump into bony walls.
Some read braille books.
Some sit around tables playing poker
with braille cards.

When the alarm goes off
they scramble to their marks.
One is trained to whisper in my ear
from in my ear, "Life goes on.
Where Hiroshima had been
Hiroshima is again."
One chirps the same four words:
"Remember flowers, music, kisses."

Sometimes a leg pops out of my ear,
kicks off the car radio. I hear
whispers: "Open a window,
listen to the birds."
Sometimes a tiny head
pokes out a nostril, then tiny hands

reach up yanking down the shades
of my eyelids.

They get exhausted,
they work in shifts.
One team sleeps,
the other team puts out fires.
I can feel them filing past
each other. One squad clipping on helmets,
the other squad plopping
onto bunks.

Without them, who knows what?
Each morning when I wake
I feel them getting ready.
Doing their little calisthenics.
Rehearsing their lines.
Practicing sword fighting
with their white canes.

On a Weekend Visit, I Drink My Coffee Downstairs and Watch a Morning Show about Pottery with My Eighty-Five-Year-Old Mother

How many mornings are you given
to comment on vases and bowls
made of clay by a blind man with no hands
using his bare feet to offer the world
something useful, even beautiful?
To hear the old woman on her chair say,
"That one is pretty," to answer, "yes,
I agree." To see her every fifteen minutes
hobble on a stick to the bathroom.
To fill her in, each time she returns,
on what she missed: "He was born
that way. He's made pottery since
age five. He says his feet have their own
intelligence." To hear her say,
"Isn't it remarkable?" To peek over
at bald spots through thinning white
hair, noticing how she pulls a blanket
up to her chin, how her mouth falls
open and her breathing deepens.
To watch her eyes eventually close,
thin blue-green veins on her eyelids
as her head tilts back and the mouth
widens. To let her snooze as the
show ends and a quiet snoring begins.
To turn off the TV and hold yourself
back from touching her, kissing her
forehead. To study every line in the

slack cheeks, realizing you've always
been coming to this morning. To almost
remember something that maybe
got lost, as though this were the first
face you'd ever see.

The Last Leaf

Who can blame it
for not wanting to let go?

Days of sun on its face.
Days of rain on its tongue.
Memory of another leaf's skin
on its skin.

Does the tree speak leaf,
whisper

> *All the stars in the sky will be yours*

but the tiny fingers and toes
just tighten their grip?

Snow, sleet, hail
don't dissuade it.

Every day I see it,
clinging,
stubborn,

and the tree, like a god,
noticing me watching
shrugs its shoulders,

a little embarrassed,
a little inspired

by something so in love
with life.

Space

When I die I bequeath the space I occupy
to more space—the space that all my life
follows me around bouncing off the line
that defines the shape I am,
since the shape of any thing is the shape
a line makes around it.
                        To that space—

that everywhere I walk parts on each side
of me like an ocean and lurks waiting
for its chance to rush in, the way my dog
sniffs at my heels in the kitchen
always hoping for the dropped potato chip—

                I invite to play,
swallow, hoard, do whatever hungry space
around us desires and does
with more space.
                I always knew it was there

since I was born but I pretend
I'm not aware. It tries so hard
to be invisible. It holds its breath.

I've been caught by friends
talking to it so it looks like I'm talking
to myself. "Be patient," I whisper.
"Hang in there, it could be any time now,"
I say.
            Usually, I just keep my mouth shut
as it slides silky hands all over my body.

Hearing

Today I used more than my ears.

The ceiling fan spoke of propellers
and blades of a boat.

The water glass on the nightstand
whispered of the ocean,
its false memory of waves.

The toothbrush spoke in tongues
of gums and the fear of garlic.

The stone spoke with regret
of not being able to float.

The blades of grass all said the same thing
in unison, as if they'd rehearsed:
thirst, thirst, thirst.

The unmade bed said
look how funny orgasms make
people's faces.

The stars said they're still waiting
for their real names, keep trying.

The bored clock did its best impersonation
of the dull thud of an instant dying.

The ugliest places on my body told me
they feel the most pleasure,

being loneliest,
which I already knew.

And resting on a quilt on her chest,
my mother's wrinkled hands
spoke of what they've held:
coffee cups, countless cantaloupes,
doorknobs and dust rags.

They kept adding to the list,
rambling,
as if they'd waited my entire life
for me to finally listen:

my dead father's strong hands,
pencils,
bars of soap sudsing my newborn flesh...

Feeding My Mother Jell-O in the Hospital

I will not distort things
like trying to make music sound better
by playing it louder. 2 a.m. Balancing
small red cubes on the plastic spoon
her open mouth strains for. Guiding
the spoon carefully the way she,
no doubt, once fed me
in a high chair. Looking at her
lying there, letting myself see
what comes of us. Strangeness
of being temporary. Relishing
the wordless, muffled click
of teeth closing on the plastic spoon inside her lips.

The Death Catcher

He lost the device all humans have behind their forehead. Like a furnace filter sifting dander and dust or an oil filter in a car straining gunk and debris—a death catcher. He serviced it regularly, removed it, cleaned off mangled soldiers, murder victims, car crash fatalities bunched up and snagged there. Maybe he misplaced it. We only get one. Now the little girl, raped and dismembered, the man reads about on the front page as he eats his Cheerios, gets in—ruining his breakfast. Later that day at work, he learns why the secretary is out: her son crushed by a tractor—ruining his lunch.

For a while, he manages. Anyone can handle a few. But soon he starts feeling heavy. Days and nights pass. With nothing to separate things out he fills up. Sometimes he can't move. He hardly eats or sleeps, all the weeping, those screams. The filter made life so much easier, allowed him to forget. He actually once felt good about clouds and trees and even other people on the street.

His time now is spent finding new ways of surviving without the device. And shuffling the bodies, trying to make room—a nook here, a corner there—for the endless depositing of starved Africans, tumor-covered babies, the shriveled mother in the nursing home who just last night stopped breathing.

Eternity

He thinks of its fabric
as something like orange fringes
of a fraying sunset.
Or a long black ribbon of migrating birds.
But in a string of cars
stopped by a train
as the sun disappears,
a city bus, its inside lights coming on,
idles.
And two strangers seated together
suddenly glow in a window,
their shoulders gently touching.

The Captured Angel Comments on My Future Self

One day he'll come back to warn you
how half-alive you've been.
He'll say joy is a bird
that hovers above your head
waiting to be noticed,
happiness is the small drab shrub
in your front yard you walk past
every day but don't see.
Something like that.
You'll ask why he's talking so fast.
He'll say he's breaking the rules
by telling you all this and has
to hurry forward again. You'll ask
if he can be more specific;
you like quasi-mystical metaphors
as much as anyone, but
they don't quite cut it.
He'll say he's probably already
in trouble. You'll offer one of your
famous martinis. He'll be tempted
(some things never change).
Your face will be different
but you'll recognize yourself.
Then—*poof*—he'll be gone.
You'll understand why he came:
The eyes were still half-alive.
Okay, maybe slightly more than half.

Dear Specter, One More Thing

Is each star a hole
a soul made
going up into heaven?

Are tears the sweat of vision?

Is that formaldehyde
behind my earlobes
or are my nostrils being ornery?

Was that a rescue boat
in my father's pneumonia lungs
that was torpedoed when he quivered
in his coma at the end?

And those stars—
is each the shiny head of a bolt
where a god screws the world
tighter to the beyond?

Acknowledgments

Grateful acknowledgment is made to the editors of the following publications, in which some of the poems in this collection first appeared, some in altered versions:

The Bacon Review: "Cancer Clinic," "Trying to Name It," "Teresa's World" and "On This Earth"
Blood Lotus Journal: "Upon Discovering My Daughter's Tattoo"
The Coachella Review: "The Captured Angel Comments on Death"
Country Dog Review: "As the Gods Booby-Trap Love"
E.T.A. Journal: "Space"
Exit 7: "The Sweat Mark" and "Hearing"
Faultline: "Show and Tell" and "Blind Hopes"
The Frank Martin Review: "The Captured Angel Sings a Psalm of Beholding"
The Georgia Review: "In Praise of Surrealism" and "In Praise of the Ordinary"
Gingerbread House Literary Magazine: "The Death Catcher"
Hawaii Pacific Review: "Death and Birth"
Hospital Drive Magazine: "Sixth Birthday: The Transparent Model Man"
lluminations: "The Only Thing I Ever Stole"
In Touch Magazine: "Eternity," "The Captured Angel Comments on Communion" and "The Captured Angel Comments on Blame"
Journal of Kentucky Studies: "Theophany" and "The Last Leaf"
The McGuffin: "Siste Viator"
Naugatuck River Review: "I Drive through a Blizzard for a Cup of Tea"
Rosebud: "Tips from an Ant"

Silhouette: "Early Lesson"
Spry Literary Journal: "The Captured Angel Comments on Boredom"
Stone Voices: "Theophany" and "The Last Leaf"
Wild Violet Magazine: "The Artist"
Wordpeace: "Noumenon"
The Write Room: "Sweetness," and "Dear Specter, One More Thing"

"The Secret Power" appeared in *The Function of Sadness*, winner of the 2015 Slipstream Press Poetry Chapbook Competition.

"Siste Viator" was reprinted in *The Evening Street Review*.

About the Author

Neil Carpathios is the author of three previous full-length poetry collections: *Beyond the Bones* (FutureCycle Press, 2009), *At the Axis of Imponderables* (winner of the Quercus Review Press Book Award, 2007), and *Playground of Flesh* (Main Street Rag, 2006). He is also the author of three chapbooks, all of which have won national competitions, most recently *The Function of Sadness* (Slipstream Press, 2015). An anthology he edited, *Every River on Earth: Writing from Appalachian Ohio* (Ohio University Press), was released in 2015. He teaches at Shawnee State University in Portsmouth, Ohio.